Real World MATH

Math in Action: Real People, Cool Jobs, Exciting Careers!

Bring math to life with **200 real-world problems** encountered in 20 fascinating careers. Just like a field trip, but a lot more practical, this book takes students out into the field where they execute a search-and-rescue mission, conduct a symphony orchestra, manage an artisanal bakery, plan a Native American powwow, run a horse therapy center, trek across the country, rescue abandoned animals, and a lot more!

Linked to math standards and paired with step-by-step solutions, this book brings students up close and personal with math in the real world. Students will quickly discover that math is essential for them to follow their dreams.

Math is everywhere—let's explore it together!

Marya Washington Tyler is a best-selling author who thoroughly enjoyed teaching math to elementary and middle school students in Wisconsin, Idaho, Washington, and Alaska. She continues to bring math to life for students around the world and is the author of several Prufrock titles including *It's Alive! The Funniest Math Book Ever!*, *Real Life Math Mysteries*, and *On the Job Math Mysteries!*

Real World

MATH

AN ANSWER TO THE QUESTION
"WHAT WILL WE EVER USE THIS FOR?"

MARYA WASHINGTON TYLER

Routledge
Taylor & Francis Group

NEW YORK AND LONDON

Designed cover image: Marya Tyler, 2026

First published 2026

by Routledge
605 Third Avenue, New York, NY 10158

and by Routledge
4 Park Square, Milton Park, Abingdon, Oxon, OX14 4RN

Routledge is an imprint of the Taylor & Francis Group, an informa business

ISBN: 9781032496139 (pbk)
ISBN: 9781003397700 (ebk)

DOI: 10.4324/9781003397700

Typeset in Felt Tip Roman, Stone Sans, A Caslon Pro
by Deanta Global Publishing Services, Chennai, India

Special thanks to the wonderfully kind people
who shared their lives for this book.

Contents

Preface

Yes, I knew I should be teaching my students real math from the real world. The NCTM recommended it, and the state standards were clear. The trouble was, most of the "real world math" I found wasn't that real. The questions would be like, "If a carpenter wanted to make a…"

I wondered, "Why doesn't someone go ask people for the math they really use?"

Then I thought, "Why don't I?"

CONTENTS & STANDARDS

3		**ADVENTURE TREKKER**
	1.	subtraction, temperature
	2.	multiply by ½
	3.	multiply by decimal
	4.	ounces/pounds, divide with decimal answer
	5.	simple multiply
	6.	add decimals
	7.	add decimals
Challenge	8.	2-step division with decimal, days in months
	9.	simple addition
4		**RESTAURANT OWNER**
	1.	multiply money, subtract money
	2.	2-step problem, multiply money
	3.	2-step problem, subtraction
	4.	2-step problem, change fraction to decimal
	5.	multiplying by fraction
Challenge	6.	3-step, multiplying
5		**BIRD BIOLOGIST**
	1.	2-step question, minutes/hours
	2.	3-step question, minutes/hours
	3.	3-step question, minutes/hours
	4.	ratio
Challenge	5.	subtract a negative number
	6.	ratio, fraction to percent
	7.	ratio, fraction to percent
	8.	ratio, fraction to percent
6		**ANIMAL SHELTER MANAGER**
	1.	divide decimal by 10, round to nearest tenth
	2.	multiply
	3.	multiply
	4.	divide
Challenge	5.	divide decimal, analyze rounding to nearest tenth

	4.	rate, miles/min to miles/hour, rounding
	5.	rate, miles/min to miles/hour, rounding
	6.	rate, miles/min to miles/hour, rounding
	(Questions 4–6 can promote discussion on rounding.)	
11	**SEARCH AND RESCUER**	
	1.	use formula, distance = rate ∗ time
	2.	use formula, distance = rate ∗ time
	3.	divide, round to nearest tenth
	4.	multistep, minutes to what decimal part of an hour
	5.	multistep, divide decimals
	6.	easy conversion to nautical miles
	7.	divide
Challenge	8.	2-step, divide, decimal hours to minutes
	9.	divide by decimal
	10.	add, nautical time
12	**ALPACA FARMER**	
	1.	show percent as a decimal, multiply by decimal
	2.	multiply by decimal
Challenge	3.	multistep, change decimal to fraction
	4.	2-step, subtract decimals
	5.	easy multiply, analyze answer
	6.	multiply by decimal
	7.	divide decimal by 2
	8.	divide by decimal, round
13	**TRIBAL PLANNER**	
	1.	2-step problem, multiply by easy decimal
	2.	convert cu yd/ cu ft, divide, round to whole
	3.	multiply decimals, round to whole
14	**SKI RACE COORDINATOR**	
	1.	temperature difference, negative number
	2.	multiply
	3.	ounce/gallon, rounding sense
	4.	divide, rounding sense
	5.	divide

	6.	multiply by decimal, round to nearest ten
Challenge	7.	subtract decimals, compare
	8.	time, minutes/seconds, subtract decimals
	9.	ounces/pound
	10.	multiply by fraction
	11.	2-step, rounding sense
15		**ORGANIC COMPOSTERS**
	1.	2 step, find percent of, multiply by decimal
Challenge	2.	multistep, add/subtract/multiply decimals
	3.	subtract decimals
	4.	convert one cu yd to cu ft
	5.	division
	6.	divide by decimal
	7.	divide, interpret decimal remainder
	8.	divide, interpret decimal remainder
16		**TALL SHIPS CAPTAIN**
Challenge	1.	rate formula, simple algebra, add time
Challenge	2.	rate formula, simple algebra
	3.	divide, round to nearest hundredth
	4.	comprehension
	5.	divide, reduce fraction
Challenge	6.	multiply fractions
Challenge	7.	multiply fractions
Challenge	8.	subtract fractions, divide decimal
17		**GUITAR SHOP OWNER**
	1.	subtract mixed number
Challenge	2.	add, subtract fractions, analyze rounding
	3.	multiply by decimal
	4.	multiply mixed number times 2
	5.	multiply mixed number times 2
	6.	multiply decimal times 2
	7.	fraction to decimal
	8.	decimal to fraction
	9.	multiply by decimal

Why Math Is Cool

- Mathematics is universal. Eight plus six is fourteen wherever you are. Different languages use different words for numbers, but the results are the same everywhere.

- Mathematics is pure. It's the same today as it was in the beginning.

- Mathematics is discovered, not invented.[1] Mathematics is still being discovered.

- The universe is based on number. The difference between an atom of gold and an atom of lead is basically the number of protons.[2]

- Doing math makes your brain quicker and sharper. The brain, just like a muscle, gets stronger with use. Learning forms connections between neurons, and that increases the mass of your brain.[3]

- Statistically, it has been shown that people who take more math courses in high school make more money.[4]

- Most animals have some sense of math.[5] Some spiders count their prey. Some ants count their steps.[6] Day-old chicks add and subtract.[7]

1 Inquibox. (n.d.). *12 famous mathematicians and their discoveries*. Retrieved from: https://inquibox.com/11-famous-mathematicians-and-their-discoveries

2 Study.com. (n.d.). *Transmutation in Alchemy | Overview & Possibility*. Retrieved from : https://study.com/academy/lesson/transforming-lead-into-gold-alchemy-transmutation.html

3 Papillion. (2023, October 18). *Your Brain on Math*. Mathnasium. Retrieved from : www.mathnasium.com/math-centers/papillion/news/your-brain-math

4 Doug Campbell. (2024). *More Math = Higher Wages + Lower Unemployment, Says Cleveland Fed Study*. Federal Reserve Bank of Cleveland. Retrieved from: www.clevelandfed.org/collections/press-releases/2013/pr-20131101-more-math-higer-wages-lower-unemployment

5 Jordana Cepelewicz. (2021, August 9). *Animals Count and Use Zero. How Far Does Their Number Sense Go?* Quanta Magazine. Retrieved from: www.quantamagazine.org/animals-can-count-and-use-zero-how-far-does-their-number-sense-go-20210809

6 Leander. (2022, May 25). *Can Animals Count?* Mathnasium: The Math Learning Center: Retrieved from www.mathnasium.com/math-centers/leander/news/can-animals-count-42519971

7 ASTC Science World Society. (2014). Chickens Can Do Math. www.scienceworld.ca/stories/chickens-can-do-math

1

Kealy White

BAKERY MANAGER

Kealy White is general manager of the Ashland Baking Company in Ashland, Wisconsin.

"I started baking when I was just out of college, when the bakery first opened, and I still spend lots of time in the kitchen. It's a very mathematical job, really."

"We use the metric system, because it's way easier to increase or decrease recipe sizes when you're working in grams and kilograms, instead of cups and ounces. Grams and kilograms are multiples of ten, but a cup is divided into eight ounces. Multiplying by ten in your head is a lot easier than multiplying by eight."

"Today I found a new brownie recipe I want to try out. We'll make a small batch first, just enough to fill a 9″ x 13″ pan. If it turns out great, we'll expand it for our sheet pans, which are 26″ x 18″."

1. "How many times larger is the sheet pan than the small batch pan?"

DOI: 10.4324/9781003397700-1

"Well, the brownies turned out terrific, so I've converted the recipe to weight (grams) instead of volume (cups, tablespoons, teaspoons). Now, let's scale it up in size. There are 1,000 grams in 1 kilogram."

EBONY CHOCOLATE BROWNIES				
Question No.	INGREDIENTS	Amount 1 batch	Amount 16 batches	
			# grams	# kilograms
2.	1¼ cup dark chocolate chips	215 grams		
3.	1½ cups garbanzo beans	250 grams		
4.	2 eggs	2 eggs	eggs	—
5.	2 tablespoons cocoa powder	14.76 grams		—
6.	¼ teaspoon cinnamon	0.7 grams		—
7.	1 tablespoon coconut oil	13.6 grams		—
8.	2 teaspoons vanilla extract	4.2 grams		—
9.	⅓ cup coconut sugar	60 grams		—
10.	½ teaspoon baking powder	2.5 grams		—
11.	½ teaspoon salt	3.5 grams		—
12.	½ cup confectioner's sugar for garnish	62 grams		—

"It's a busy day at the bakery. Two different departments need to put their pans in the same oven at the same time, but at different temperatures. The honey wheat bread calls for a temperature of 350 degrees F and our brownie recipe calls for 325 degrees F."

13. "What's the average of the two temperatures?"

"The sheet of brownies is out of the oven, and mmm, they smell great. We have to be very precise as we cut them—each brownie has to be just the same size. The pan is 26″ x 18″, and we need exactly 48 brownies."

14. Challenge: "If we cut each brownie 3″ wide, how long will each brownie be?"

PROBLEM-SOLVING STRATEGY: Draw a diagram.

"My dad was a math teacher. He'll be tickled to see this."

2

Joy Ratkowski

HORSE THERAPIST

"Horses are amazing!" Joy and her husband Russ own Hooves of Joy Therapeutic Riding Center, where adults and children with disabilities can experience the joy of riding horses. And here wonderful things happen!

Russ explains, "We have children come in who are upset and uncooperative. Twenty minutes later, they are listening and following directions. We have clients who are autistic, some with muscular dystrophy, multiple sclerosis, brain trauma, Down syndrome, and they leave here feeling good about themselves."

"There's a lot of math here every day. We own 22 horses, and their hooves need trimming every four weeks. Trimming costs 40 dollars per horse.

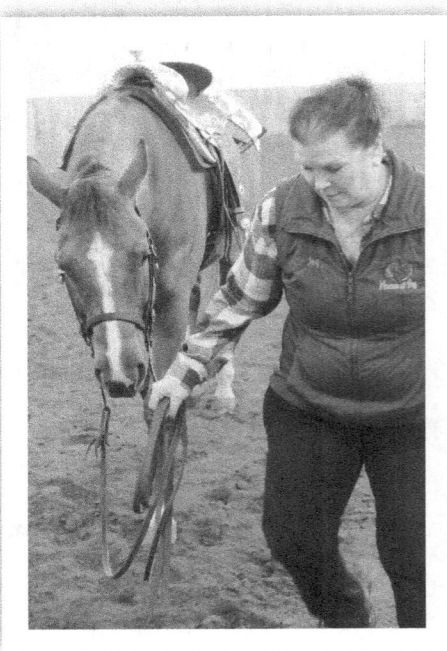

1. **"How many times are the horses' hooves trimmed per year?"** *(52 weeks)*

2. **"How much does hoof trimming cost us per year?"**

"Horses drink a lot of water. Each horse drinks at least ten gallons of water a day."

3. **"Our horses drink at least how many gallons per year?"** *(365 days)*

DOI: 10.4324/9781003397700-2

"Horses eat about 2.5% of their body weight in hay per day. Our horses weigh about 1,000 pounds on average.

4. **"About how much hay should we give each horse daily?"**

5. **"About how many pounds of hay should we give out to all the horses each day?"**

6. **"About how many pounds of hay will we need for one year?"** *(365 days)*

"Each bale of hay weighs 1000 pounds."

7. **"How many bales of hay do I need to order for next year?"** *(I can only order whole bales.)*

"I want to be sure to have extra hay here, so I've decided to order 250 grass bales at $100 each, and an additional 50 alfalfa bales at $375 each."

8. **"How much will we spend on hay this year?"**

Joy adds: "Because every horse is different, we use a formula to figure out how much hay to give each of the horses. It's based on their weight... but how do you weigh a horse?"
    "You use math."

$$\frac{\text{Heart girth in inches} * \text{heart girth in inches}) * \text{body length}}{330} = \text{weight in pounds}$$

"Our sorrel horse Dolly has a girth 69 inches around, and her body length is 70 inches."

9. Challenge: "How much does Dolly weigh to the nearest pound?"

"A horse's height is measured in hands. Every 4 inches is called one hand."
Fill in the blanks below.

Breed of Horse	Average Height in Hands	Average Height in Inches
10. Clydesdale horse		68 inches
11. Shetland pony	9 hands 2 inches	
12. Quarter horse		60 inches
13. Arabian horse	14 hands 3 inches	

Joy continues: "There's an easy way to see if a horse is being given too much to eat. Measure around her heart girth in inches, and multiply that by 1.26. If the result is equal to or less than the height of the horse in inches, the horse is a healthy weight. If the result is more than the horse's height, the horse is overweight."

"Our Haflinger Penny is looking a little chubby. We measure Penny's girth and it is 44 inches. She's 13 hands and 2 inches tall."

14. **"Is Penny overweight?"** *(Show your work.)*

"The horses walk, jog, trot, lope, canter, and gallop in a circle around our arena. The circle is 90 feet across."

15. **"How far around is the circle to the nearest foot?"** *(Circumference equals pi times diameter, and pi = 3.14.)*

"A horse galloping has a stride of 4.5 feet."

16. **"How many galloping strides will a horse take in a full circle of the arena?"** *(Round to the nearest whole stride.)*

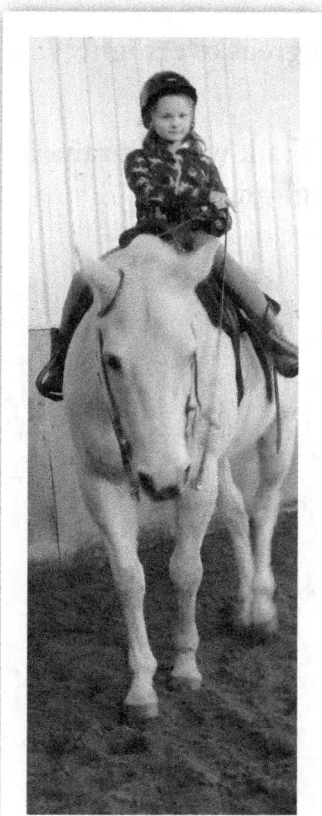

Joy says,
"The ability to control a horse under you is a wonderful feeling. It makes you believe you can do anything!"

3

Shane Peltonen

ADVENTURE TREKKER

In the past ten years, Shane Peltonen has hiked most of the United States, outside of Alaska and Hawaii.

There was the 1,000-mile Arizona Trail, where he woke up to find ten scorpions crawling on top of his sleeping bag. A little later, he almost stepped on a rattlesnake.

On the 550-mile Superior Hiking Trail, Shane went to sleep with the temperature 60 degrees F and woke up covered in snow. In June!

1. The temperature dropped at least how many degrees overnight?

Next, Shane hiked the 4,800-mile North Country Trail, where it rained every day for over a month. And he was struck by lightning!

DOI: 10.4324/9781003397700-3

2. If it rained ½ inch of rain every day for 33 days, how much did it rain?

Undaunted, Shane set out on the 1,200-mile Ice Age Trail. The mosquitoes were so thick the sky was black. One day, his legs were covered in more than a thousand ticks!

Then he headed out on the 300-mile Long Trail in Vermont, where the mud was so deep that when he fell in a puddle, it was a struggle to get out.

Then Shane hiked the entire 3,200-mile Continental Divide Trail, where he stood face to face with a grizzly bear, fell off a glacier, broke his hand, and tore his shoulder. Shane kept on walking.

"Water is life to a trekker. Through the Great Basin desert in Nevada, I had to carry 8 liters of water. Even so, I only allowed myself to drink every couple of hours—not even big drinks. All that water adds a lot of weight."

3. "How many ounces of water was I carrying? A liter of water weighs 35.2 ounces."

4. "Sixteen ounces is one pound. How many pounds is that?"

Next Shane hiked the 550-mile Colorado Trail, where he was caught in hail as big as golf balls, and woke up one day covered in ants.

Ever onward, then Shane hiked the 2,650-mile Pacific Crest Trail, where the wildfire smoke was so thick that it was sometimes dark in the middle of the day.

And then the longest trail of all—the 5,000-mile south route and the 1,800-mile north segment of the American Discovery Trail. He was swarmed by biting horse-flies, blown over by a tornado, and chased by vicious dogs. The temperature was over 115 degrees F for two straight months.

What does he carry with him? Shane says, "I eat about two pounds of food a day. Most of what I carry is nuts, seeds, dark chocolate, peanut butter, dried fruits, cold cereals, nutrition bars, graham crackers, and (my favorite) fig bars."

5. **"How many pounds of food do I need to carry for 15 days?"**

"And then there's the weight of my gear."

my empty backpack	2 pounds
my shelter: just a tarp and groundsheet	1 pound
extra clothing, hat, coat	2 pounds
water purification system	0.5 pounds
insect repellant, nail clippers, bandages, etc.	2.5 pounds
electrolyte packets, vitamins/minerals	0.5 pounds
phone, batteries, headlamp, satellite messenger	1.5 pounds
multitool, repair tape, scissors	0.5 pounds

6. **"How many pounds of gear am I carrying?"**

7. **"If I'm heading out with 8 liters of water and 15 days' food, how many total pounds will I be carrying?"**

"Math? I'm doing that stuff in my head all day long."

"Like on the American Discovery Trail… In the first 16 weeks, I have been traveling 2,500 miles, keeping a steady pace of 23 miles a day. But now it's July 1st, I'm in Kansas, and it's 120 degrees F. I need to get up and over the Sierra Nevada Mountains before the snow comes in mid-October. That's 2,400 more miles of hiking!"

8. Challenge: "Will I make it over the mountains in time?"
(Show your math to prove your answer.)

What's next? Shane is gearing up to hike the Pinhoti/Appalachian Trail—2,550 miles through 15 states…and he's doing it one footstep at a time.

9. "When I finish, how many miles will I have hiked in all?"

"You name it, I've slept there. I've slept on pews in churches…on the floor of an old barn… I've slept in deer stands…in culverts (not a good place to be in a flash flood!). When it's snowing and the wind is blowing 80 miles an hour, even a vault toilet looks like a mansion!"

"Why do I hike?
It's a good way to see the country."

4

Aquiles Garcia Cardoso

RESTAURANT OWNER

Aquiles owns Taqueria La Monarca. "I named it La Monarca for the monarch butterflies which fly 2,300 miles from here on Lake Superior to winter in Michoacán, Mexico, my home town."

"It takes a lot of math to run a restaurant, even to determine the prices to put on the menu. A box of steaks costs me $800. The box contains 80 pieces, which I sell at $14.99 apiece."

1. "Subtracting our cost, how much money do we make on one box?"

"For $30 of ground beef, I make 100 tacos and charge $3.75 apiece."

2. "How much money do we make?"

"But I have to take away another $80 for the cheese and $50 for the lettuce."

3. "How much do I have left?"

"If a customer requests five orders of extra tomato, I charge $5 extra. But I only spend $2, so I have made three dollars."

4. "How much do I make on each order of extra tomatoes?"

DOI: 10.4324/9781003397700-4

"If somebody wants three orders of sour cream, I spend a dollar and make two dollars. You have to do that because if you have any product you don't make any money on, you will not be able to pay your rent and insurance, buy equipment and furniture, fix things, pay your employees."

"A starting chef here makes $18.00 an hour. After 40 hours of work in one week, we give overtime pay. I pay time and a half for overtime."

5. **"How much does a starting chef get per overtime hour?"**

6. **Challenge: "If a starting chef works 48 hours in a week, what is his pay?"**

"We have four working in the kitchen and two servers and a busboy, and I supervise. If I have to do dishes, I don't have any trouble with that. If somebody comes in looking for the boss, they will find me doing dishes. If I have to help with the chairs, I love it. And I have to teach the kitchen staff my menu. Even though I supervise, I'm basically a worker like everybody."

"This business plan is very good for everybody, because if I made it an expensive place, there are a lot of people who don't have a lot of money. If I have ten dollars in my pocket, I can come and eat. It's really good for everybody."

"I only went to school one year, when I was five years old. My family didn't have money to buy books and shoes. I decided I would come to the U.S. and work very hard. At age 13, I came to the U.S. by myself. Somebody gave me a ride. At that time, it was all legal—June 22, 2005. I came with nothing. Now I speak two languages, own a restaurant, and provide jobs for several people."

5

Ted Gostomski

BIRD BIOLOGIST

To hear a bird singing in the distance, and know what kind of bird it is just by listening… How many people can do that? Ted Gostomski can.

As coordinator of songbird monitoring for the Great Lakes Inventory and Monitoring Network, Ted surveys the rise and fall of bird populations in nine different national parks, identifying each of 100 species by listening for their songs.

"I've been studying birds since I was 12 years old. The same way kids know their parent's voice in a crowd, I've learned the unique pattern, tone, and pitch of each species' song."

Ted says, "Want to come with me? You'll have to get up early. We want to be at the first listening point a half hour before sunrise. Here in northern Wisconsin, the sun rises at 5:09 a.m. on June 14th. It takes me 20 minutes to get ready, 35 minutes to drive to the park, and 45 minutes to hike in the dark to the listening point."

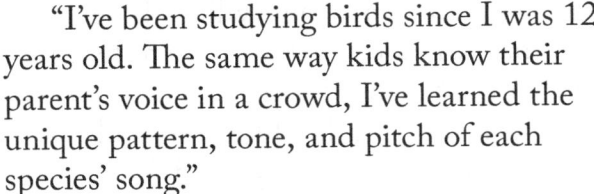

1. **"What time do I want to arrive?"**

2. **"What time do I have to get up?"**

DOI: 10.4324/9781003397700-5

"I'll stand there in the dim light, listening to everything and writing it down, but usually the people I'm with are just being bitten by mosquitos. After ten minutes, we'll hike to the next listening spot, and I'll record what I hear. We'll keep going until four hours after sunrise."

3. "If it's a 45-minute hike back to my vehicle from the last listening point, what time would I get home?"

"One way we examine bird populations is by guilds. There are four diet guilds: Frugivores eat fruit, granivores eat seeds, insectivores eat mostly insects, and omnivores eat everything. Check out this data we collected over three years."

Population Density Trends for Landbirds at Mississippi National River and Recreation Area			
Guild Category	**Guild (Number of Species)**	**Example Species**	**Slope**
Diet	Frugivore (4)	Cedar waxwing	+1.73
	Granivore (2)	American goldfinch	+4.91
	Insectivore (13)	Starling	−0.42
	Omnivore (6)	American crow	+0.17
Forage substrate	Air (2)	Tree swallow	+0.66
	Bark (5)	Downy woodpecker	−0.42
	Shrub/low canopy (12)	Northern cardinal	+0.19
	Upper canopy (3)	Rose-breasted grosbeak	+0.01
Habitat	Open grassland (2)	Red-winged blackbird	+8.00
	Agricultural/shrub (8)	Mourning dove	−0.47
	Urban (8)	Rock dove	−0.26
	Woodland (15)	Yellow warbler	+0.09
Migrant status	Continental (4)	Bluebird	−0.69
	Neotropical (6)	Baltimore oriole	+0.54
	Permanent (10)	Black-capped chickadee	+0.98
From "Songbird Monitoring in the Great Lakes Network Parks," provided by National Park Service			

4. **"What is the ratio of frugivore species to omnivores?"**

"We also look at where the birds find their food—do they pluck insects out of the air, or off the bark of trees, or do they pick seeds and berries from the ground, in shrubs, or in trees? And where do they live—open grassland, wetland, scrub, woodland, or cities? Slope in the table tells how the species populations are changing. It's measured in number of birds per square kilometer each year."

5. **Challenge:**
   "What is the difference in the slope of grassland birds and urban birds?"

"Finally, we look at where they go in the winter—do they stay here, migrate within the continental United States, or migrate to the tropics?"

6. **"What percent of species are permanent residents all year?"**

7. **"What percent of species migrate within the continental U.S.?"**

8. **"What percent of species migrate to the tropics?"**

"Learning the songs was challenging, but it has opened up new ways of looking at the land when I'm hiking or even just walking in my neighborhood. When migrating birds return in the spring, hearing their familiar songs is like reconnecting with old friends."

[Editor's note: Check out the free app *Merlin*, which can give you information about the birds you hear!]

6
Molly Lawton
ANIMAL SHELTER MANAGER

"Every year, more than 700 animals are adopted from the Chequamegon Humane Association—dogs, cats, rats, guinea pigs, rabbits, pigs. Once even a tarantula. We see animals at their worst, and do whatever we can to help them become adoptable. I think it's the most meaningful thing I've ever done in my life."

"This morning, we had a sweet little black-and-white mixed breed brought in. We named him Snoopy. Like lots of puppies we get, he had a big round belly, indicating his intestines were full of worms. Treatment involves giving one milliliter of liquid deworming medicine for every 10 pounds of dog weight. Snoopy weighs 34.6 pounds."

1. **"How many milliliters of dewormer do I give Snoopy?"** *(Round to nearest tenth.)*

"A few weeks ago, the animal control officer brought us a scrawny gray cat that had been wandering the streets for days. He was weak, his eyes appeared sunken, and his gums were dry and sticky, so I knew he was dehydrated. Ralph weighed only 10 pounds. Giving a dehydrated cat more than 1 ounce of fluid per pound of body weight is dangerous."

2. **"How many ounces of water could I safely give Ralph?"**

DOI: 10.4324/9781003397700-6

"The tricky thing is, our syringe measures in milliliters, not ounces. One ounce of water contains 30 milliliters."

3. **"How many milliliters of water could I safely give Ralph?**

"Not long ago a brave yellow cat was brought in. Charlie showed no sign of pain, but I could tell something was wrong by the way he walked. The veterinarian discovered that Charlie had been shot in the leg. It required amputation, so Charlie came back from the vet on three legs. The vet prescribed 62.5 milligrams of Amoxicillin to prevent infection. Here's the tricky part. The medicine, being liquid, is measured in milliliters, not milligrams. The bottle says that 5 milliliters of Amoxicillin equals 400 milligrams."

4. **"So, 1 milliliter of Amoxicillin equals how many milligrams?"**

5. **Challenge: "Now help me find the correct dosage to give Charlie to the nearest tenth of a milliliter. It's better to give him too little, rather than too much."**

"Charlie was soon after adopted by a wonderful family."

"Animals are so smart. They just communicate differently. Take care of your animals. Know that they love you even though they can't tell you directly. We're the voice for animals that can't speak for themselves."

7

Nathan Mitchell

ORCHESTRA CONDUCTOR

"Have you ever thought it would be fun to be the conductor of an orchestra, waving your baton in time to the music? Well, it's not quite so simple. As conductor, my job is to keep 4 French horns, 3 trumpets, 3 trombones, 1 tuba, 3 clarinets, 2 bassoons, 2 flutes, 2 oboes, 10 violins, 5 violas, 5 cellos, 3 basses, and 1 timpani all playing the right note at the right tempo and the right volume in the right mood at the same time!"

1. **"Horns, trumpets, trombones and tuba are brass instruments. The brass section is what fraction of the orchestra?"** *(Reduce the fraction.)*

2. **"Clarinets, bassoons, flutes, and oboes are woodwind instruments. The woodwind section is what fraction of the orchestra?"**

3. **"Violins, violas, cellos, and basses are string instruments. The string section is what fraction of the orchestra?"**

4. **"Is the string section more or less than half the orchestra?"**

"My left hand guides the orchestra with volume, emotion, and expression. The baton in my right hand keeps the beat. When we're playing a song written for 60 beats per minute, I beat the baton one beat every second."

DOI: 10.4324/9781003397700-7

Chequamegon Symphony Orchestra

5. "If the song is written for 180 beats per minute, how many beats is that per second?"

6. "And if the song is written at 90 beats per minute, how many beats is that per second?"

7. "Because it's not easy to think of half a beat per second, I think 'How many beats every two seconds?' At 90 beats/minute, how many beats every two seconds?"

"This chart shows basic notes when there are 4 beats per measure. A half note doesn't mean half a beat. It means half the measure, which is 2 beats."

8. "Four eighth-notes are how many total beats?"

9. Challenge: "How many sixteenth notes would fit in the rest of this measure?"

	half	2 beats
	quarter	1 beat
	eighth	½ beat
	sixteenth	¼ beat

"Tchaikovsky's original symphony, written in 1872, is divided into four movements. **Knowing that each bar is about one second long, determine the length of each movement to the nearest minute.**"

10. Movement I—486 bars

11. Movement II—179 bars

12. Movement III—481 bars

13. Movement IV—993 bars

"I have fun while I'm conducting. If I'm too serious, I know I'm not going to enjoy my time, and I'm pretty sure the musicians are not going to enjoy their time. If we have an enjoyable rehearsal, they'll get better naturally."

8
Amaris
FOOD SHELF MANAGER

Pineapples, broccoli, salmon, walnuts, sweet potatoes, milk, cheese, snacks—the food is all free at the BRICK! Every year, volunteers distribute thousands of pounds of donated food to hundreds of families in need. Amaris is in charge of picking up all the food, sorting it, storing it, and making sure it's distributed fairly. That takes math.

"Right now the BRICK is serving an average total of 450 households per month in four locations: South Shore, Ashland, Cable, and Mellen. South Shore serves an average of 24 households."

1. **"What percent of our donated food should go to the South Shore food shelf?"** *(Round to the nearest whole percent.)*

"The Ashland food shelf averages 278 households."

2. **"What percent of our donated food should go to Ashland?"** *(Round to the nearest whole percent.)*

"We rescue produce that would have gone to the landfill. It's a win-win-win situation. Grocery stores and bakeries that give us their extra food win, because they get a government tax break. Hundreds of families win, because they get fresh fruits, vegetables, bread, and dairy. Happy pigs, chickens, and sheep win, because all the food that is not able to be given away before it spoils goes to their farm. Everybody wins."

DOI: 10.4324/9781003397700-8

"The donations we receive have a 'best by' date printed on the label, but that doesn't mean they aren't still good. Using the guidelines in the chart below, I can determine whether or not to keep these donations, which we received on April 12th, 2026, or to send them to the farms."

REFRIGERATED DONATIONS SAFETY CHECK

#	Donation	Product can be safely consumed past:	"Best by" date we see on the label	Donation can be safely distributed until this date:	Keep? Y or N
3.	Yogurt	10 days	April 21, 2026		
4.	Cream cheese	2 weeks	March 24, 2026		
5.	Hard cheese	6 months	October 17, 2025		
6.	Soft cheese	1 week	April 7, 2026		
7.	Challenge: Eggs in shell	4 weeks	March 18, 2026		
8.	Butter	2 months	February 28, 2025		

"We need to supply a whole lot of statistics to the U.S. government, because the government supplies about one-fourth of the food we give away."

"For example, we are asked to calculate the average number of children per household served."

9. **"Use the chart below and round to the nearest tenth."**

(Hint: "children per household" can be written "children/household" and the "/" symbol always means "divide the top by the bottom.")

BRICK	Households	Children 0–17	Adults 18–60	Adults over 60	Total People
TOTAL	3,313	2,087	3,921	2,002	8,011

"We serve quite a few homeless folks…people living in their cars…living at a friend's…living under bridges. We can't feed all of the people all of the time, but it helps. I'm super grateful that free food shelves are a thing in this country. It's not the case in every country."

9

Addie Arens

HEAD LIBRARIAN

Librarians don't use math... Right?

Addie responds: "Well, no! As director of the Drummond Public Library, I use a lot of math."

"Today I'm budgeting for the coming year. I have $6,500 to spend on collections. How do I decide what to buy?"

"I look at what kinds of things were checked out this year."

1. **"Help me find out what percent of the total checkouts were HARDCOVER BOOKS."** *(Round to the nearest whole percent.)*

2. **"What percent were OTHER BOOKS?"** *(Round to the nearest whole percent.)*

3. **"What percent were LARGE PRINT BOOKS?"** *(Round to the nearest whole percent.)*

4. **"Based on this information, how much of the $6,500 should I spend on BOOKS in general?"**

CHECKOUTS THIS YEAR	
AUDIOBOOK	151
BLU-RAY	37
BOARD BOOK	52
BOARD GAME	1
BOOK HARDCOVER	3,008
BOOK LARGE PRINT	80
BOOK OTHER	403
COMPUTER SOFTWARE	699
DVD	10
EQUIPMENT	32
GRAPHIC WORKS	104
KITS	5
MAGAZINES	12
MUSIC CD	5
TOTAL	4,599

DOI: 10.4324/9781003397700-9

"I keep a record of how many people hold a library card from Drummond Library each month. I like to see more and more people taking advantage of the library."

5. **"Fill out the CHANGE column below with the amount of increase or decrease in people checking out materials from the previous month."**

6. **"What was the total change?"** *(indicate plus or minus)*

7. **"What was the average monthly change?"** *(Rounded to the nearest whole percent.)*

"I did not like math in school. I used to really struggle with it. Now, I handle the library budget, plus the budget for the snowmobile club, the Drummond Lake Association, the campground, and more!"

"Math isn't so hard when you get out into the real world. Learn your basic math skills. You'll use them your whole life."

PATRON COUNTS		CHANGE
January	578	0
February	580	
March	596	
April	595	
May	604	
June	607	
July	611	
August	613	
September	621	
October	623	
November	625	
December	627	
TOTAL	7,280	

10

Anne Workman

STATE TROOPER

It takes a special person to be a Wisconsin State Patrol Trooper. No matter the danger involved, Anne Workman is out assisting stranded motorists, attending to the injured in car crashes, and enforcing traffic laws to keep Wisconsin highways safe. Every day is something different.

"I like being a state trooper, because I'm not a sit-behind-the-desk kind of person. State troopers have a lot of independence. We are often called upon to make split-second decisions, decisions that can mean life or death, and we use math all the time."

"Right now, I see a car approaching that is obviously speeding. I check its speed on my radar as it passes and see it's going 75 miles per hour in a 55-mph zone. I activate my lights and siren, turn around, and pursue the vehicle. Our cars are specifically designed for speed even on narrow, winding roads, and I am able to catch the vehicle a mile and a half later, after one minute."

1. **"How fast did I have to drive to catch this speeder?"**

Hint:

$$\frac{miles}{\cancel{minute}} * \frac{\cancel{minute}}{hour} = \frac{miles}{hour}$$

"On high-traffic weekends, state troopers in airplanes fly overhead and clock the speed of cars below."

DOI: 10.4324/9781003397700-10

"The pilot radios to the trooper below: 'A light green minivan was clocked traveling four miles in three minutes.' The speed limit here is 55 miles per hour."

2. **Challenge: "How fast was this person going?"**

"We need to record information for all vehicles that are speeding over 55 mph. Find each one's speed to the nearest tenth of a mile per hour, and record the number of miles over the speed limit it's traveling." Answers may vary due to rounding,)

Question No.	Vehicle description	Time to go 4 miles	Miles per hour	mph over speed limit
3.	White Chevy Bolt	3.2 minutes		
4.	Black Cadillac	3.6 minutes		
5.	Black Subaru SUV	3.4 minutes		
6.	Red BMW sedan	2.9 minutes		

"I've seen some very bad crashes. We see people at their worst, when they are totally stressed. We've got to think calmly and clearly when others can't."

"I'm blessed to be able to serve my community, and to keep our roads and communities safe."

11
Petty Officer Malcolm Venus
SEARCH AND RESCUER

The Coast Guard mission is to keep boaters safe, save lives, and ensure national security on all 3,600 square miles of Lake Superior.

It's not an easy job. Lake Superior is known for its raging storms, rapidly changing weather, 30-foot waves, and frigidly cold water. But when Coast Guard Station Bayfield receives a distress call, Petty Officer Venus jumps to the rescue.

"We just received a call from a person on shore who saw a lone kayaker capsize in the 3-foot waves. The caller said the person drifted out of sight. We need to respond immediately."

"There are no street signs on Lake Superior, so we use math to figure out how far to go (in nautical miles), how fast to go (in knots), and how long it will take us to get there (in hours)."

"This formula is very useful: distance = speed * time ."

1. **"If you know distance and time, how can you find speed?"**
   speed =

2. **"If you know distance and speed, how can you find time?"**
   time =

DOI: 10.4324/9781003397700-11

"As fast as we safely can, we boat where the kayaker was last seen, and at that spot we throw a life ring in the water, watching which way it drifts."

"While we search in an expanding square pattern (drawn below), the life ring drifts 960 yards."

"A nautical mile is longer than a regular mile. 1 NM is about 2,000 yards long."

3. **"960 yards is how far in nautical miles?"** *(Give answer to the nearest tenth.)*

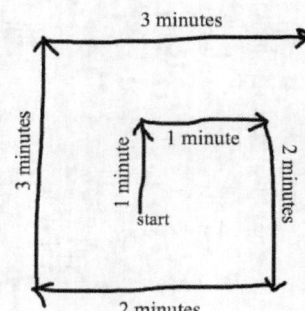

4. **"How long have we been searching?"**
   (Give the answer in hours, in decimal form.)

5. **"How fast is the life ring drifting in nautical miles/hour?"**

6. **"1 NM = 1 knot. How fast is the life ring drifting in knots?"**

"Knowing how fast and what direction the life ring drifts helps us determine the kayaker's position. From there, we proceed 10,000 yards in the direction of drift at a speed of 25 knots."

"We arrive to find a man barely clinging to his overturned kayak in the pounding waves."

7. "How many nautical miles did we travel?"

8. Challenge: "How many minutes did it take us to get there?" *(Hint: see #2)*

"The kayaker is weak and grateful to be found. We pull him out of the water, wrap him in warm blankets, and treat him for hypothermia. Meanwhile, we load his kayak onto our boat and immediately head back to base, 15 nautical miles away. He's safe on land 30 minutes later."

9. "How fast did our boat travel back to base?" *(Give answer in knots.)*

"The Coast Guard uses a 24-hour clock system. That means instead of 8:00 a.m. we say 0800 *(oh eight hundred)*. And instead of 5:00 p.m. we say 1700 *(17 hundred)*."

10. "If we received the distress call at 1230 and the mission was completed in an hour and a half, what time did we finish in nautical time?"

"I love my job—being on the water, driving the response boats, training people, and carrying out missions. I love doing what I do."

12
Abby Klema
ALPACA FARMER

Visit Suri Fina alpaca farm, and Abby will introduce you to Flash Dash, Cassidy, Kali, Rhyme, Taura, Buttercup, Autumn, Luna, McKayla, Sura, Harry, Ron, Hermione, Bane, Fawkes, Frank, Hortence, Gilphy, Primrose, Soren, Helado, Kismit, Flavia, Bell, Mozzarella, Brie, and Manchego! They all know their name, and she can tell them all apart.

"The alpacas graze on 14 acres of pasture grass, which we cut and dry for hay in the winter. An alpaca eats 1.5% of its body weight in hay every day."

1. "Frank weighs 150 pounds. How many pounds of hay does he eat each day?" *(Don't round.)*

2. "How many pounds of hay does he eat in a week?" *(Don't round.)*

"One bale of hay weighs 60 pounds."

3. **Challenge: "About how many bales of hay will Frank eat in a week?"** *(Give answer as a fraction.)*

DOI: 10.4324/9781003397700-12

"Bell is a cria (a baby alpaca) who weighed 14 pounds at birth one month ago. Healthy crias double their weight the first month. Abby's farmhand holds Bell on the scale to see how much she weighs. The farmhand weighs 178 pounds. The little coat baby Bell is wearing weighs 0.6 pounds. The scale reads 207.4 pounds."

4. "How much does baby Bell weigh?"

5. "Has she doubled her weight?"

"My husband and I shear the animals each spring. Larger male alpacas like Helado might have 9 pounds of fleece, and females like Flash Dash only 4 pounds. The median across the herd is 6.5 pounds per alpaca."

6. "How many pounds of fleece can we expect from our 27 alpacas?"

"Only 50% of the fleece is prime, and that's the fleece that is knitted into socks."

7. "How many pounds of prime fleece will we get?" *(Do not round.)*

"Each pair of alpaca-fiber socks requires 0.4 pounds of prime fleece."

8. "How many whole pairs of socks can we expect to get from the herd this spring?"

"At the end of the day, when the sun is going down, the alpacas often leap for joy, all four feet jumping at once, following one after another in a line across the field. I love my alpacas."

13

Ben Connors

Bad River Band of Lake Superior Chippewa

TRIBAL PLANNER

"For me as tribal planner, math is constant. All the projects we face have a budget and a timeline—there are wages, gas, materials. It gets complicated fast…"

"Like when we have construction projects. It would be easy for someone selling gravel to put 11 cubic yards of rock in your truck and tell you it's 15 cubic yards, but that can't happen when I purchase by weight. The truck is weighed empty and then it's weighed again after loading. That way I know I'm getting what I ordered."

"I'm looking to buy gravel for a mile of road, 22-feet wide, to be covered six inches deep."

1. **"How many cubic feet of gravel do I need?"** *(1 mile = 5,280 feet)*

2. **"A cubic yard is 3 feet x 3 feet x 3 feet. How many cubic yards do I need?"** *(Round to the nearest cubic yard.)*

"A cubic yard of gravel weighs 1.25 tons."
3. **"How many whole tons should I order?"**

DOI: 10.4324/9781003397700-13

"Everybody's math teacher in school tells you you're going to use math your whole life. They're absolutely not lying. Whether you love it or hate it, you're not going to get away from it. Absorb it. You're going to use it."

The Bad River flows into Lake Superior in far northern Wisconsin, and it is possible that it was given its name by the French explorers who encountered the river's steep waterfalls. The native people, however, like Ben Connor, think of the river as Mushkeezeebi—Medicine River. Native people are deeply connected to the land, and respect for the Creator indwells every part of their lives.

14

Rachel Frydenlund

SKI RACE COORDINATOR

The Birkebeiner is one of the longest and hardest cross-country ski races in North America. Over ten thousand skiers come to race the 50-kilometer (37-mile) trail through the dense forests of northern Wisconsin. Forty thousand spectators cheer them on. Thousands of volunteers are there to help. And it's Rachel Frydenlund's job to make sure all of the supplies are in place and accounted for, so that everyone has a good time.

Rachel says, "I need to think, 'How many bananas will ten thousand racers eat?' 'How many gallons of soup do ten thousand racers consume?' I have to order the food before we even know how many racers will sign up. Plus, the temperature on race day will affect how much food they'll eat. Once, the temperature at the start of the race was negative 13 degrees Fahrenheit!"

1. **"How many degrees below freezing was it?"**

"No matter how cold it is, skiers need water. We provide water, snacks, and electrolyte drink along the course."

DOI: 10.4324/9781003397700-14

2. "If we expect 10,000 skiers, and plan for each person to consume one seven-ounce cup of electrolyte drink, how many ounces of drink will we need?"

"I can only order by the gallon."

3. "How many gallons should I order?" *(128 fluid ounces = 1 gallon.)*

"The electrolyte drink comes dehydrated. The label says to add 36 tablets to each five-gallon bucket of water."

4. How many five-gallon buckets do I need to get?" *(Make sure your answer makes sense.)*

"There are 12 tablets in a tube."

5. "How many tubes are used per bucket?"

6. "How many tubes do I need to order?" *(Round up to the nearest ten tubes.)*

"There are nine aid stations along the route, and I need to figure out how many gallons of drink go to each aid station. This gets tricky, because I can't just divide it evenly to the nine stations. That's because people get thirstier as they go. These are the kinds of logistics I have to figure out."

Check out the chart showing all nine aid stations along the 50-kilometer route. Calculate the distances between each of them.

7. Challenge: "Which aid stations are the farthest apart?"

LOCATION	FROM START
Start	0
Timber Trail	7K
Fire Tower	11.5K
Boedecker	16.1K
Double O	20.6K
Gravel Pit	29.5K
Mosquito Brook	35.4K
Fish Hatchery	41.1K
Finish Line	50K

"We have to be sure we are ready with hot soup at the finish line when the finishers arrive. And the racers seem to get faster every year! In 1973, the first-place skier finished in 2 hours 48 minutes 16.00 seconds (2:48:16.00). Fifty years later, the first place skier finished in 2 hours 5 minutes and 39.93 seconds (2:05:39.93)."

8. "How much faster was 2023 than 1973?"

"I plan for every racer to consume 1½ portions of soup. Every portion is 16 ounces. That's a lot of pounds of soup!"

9. "How many pounds am I planning per racer?"

"I'm expecting 10,000 racers."

10. "How many pounds of soup should I order?"

"The soup comes by the case. Each case contains four 4-pound bags."

11. "How many full cases of soup should I order?"

"As soon as the Birke is over, our next event is only two weeks away: the Fat Bike Birkie… We're expecting 1,000 bicyclists. And then the Epic Bike Fest (1,000 more), then the Lumberjack World Championships (12,000 more…)."

15

Jamie Tucker and Todd Rothe

ORGANIC COMPOSTERS

BIG LAKE ORGANICS

Jamie and Todd want your apple cores, potato peelings, moldy bread, broccoli stems, and burnt toast. Why? They turn it into soil—beneficial organic soil that would otherwise have rotted in a landfill, giving off poisonous greenhouse gases.

Todd: "We take your plant-based garbage and mix it with woody materials to begin this magical process called composting. Microorganisms do the rest of the work, decomposing the materials and adding nutrients, creating a rich living soil for growing nutritious food."

Jamie: "Customers each receive a bin to collect their vegetable scraps in, and they pay us to pick it up once a week. We charge $30 a month for the first bin, and $20 a month for each additional bin we pick up. We also charge for fuel, based on how far away they live. For 20 miles, it's 15%."

1. **"Aunt Mildred lives 20 miles from Big Lakes Organics and has two bins. How much per month does Mildred pay for us to pick up her veggie scraps?"**

"We bring Mildred's full bins to our facility, and weigh them. One weighs 64.8 pounds and the other weighs 72.9 pounds. Empty, a bin weighs 20.4 pounds.

2. **Challenge: "How much material did her two bins together contain this week?"**

"To turn Mildred's scraps into soil, we need both carbon and nitrogen. Carbon-containing materials are brown, like wood shavings and dead leaves. Nitrogen materials are green, like vegetable scraps, grass, and weeds. When these two combine, their bacteria become active, and break down the pile into rich compost."

DOI: 10.4324/9781003397700-15

"Once a month, we dump all the materials we've collected into a large mixer with a scale on it. First the brown goes in (638.5 pounds today), then the green. We record the total (2,020.4 pounds today), and figure out how much green we added."

3. "How much green did we add?"

"Now the mix is shredded and piled outside in windrows. This is where the magic happens. As bacteria in the leaves chomp away at Aunt Mildred's (and other people's) veggie scraps, the pile naturally warms up. Once the pile reaches 131 degrees Fahrenheit, the harmful stinky bacteria have died, and only helpful bacteria are left! Now we have to keep the pile above 131 degrees for 15 days. This is tricky, because if its temperature goes above 160 degrees, the pile can spontaneously combust! We make sure that doesn't happen!"

"Finally, the product is tested to make sure it is good clean compost, and run through a screen to give to our customers. The finished compost is sold at grocery stores in one-cubic-foot bags."

4. "How many cubic-foot bags can we fill from one cubic yard of compost?"

"One cubic yard weighs about 1000 pounds."

5. "How heavy is a one-cubic-foot bag of compost?" (*to the nearest pound*)

"The windrows are measured in cubic yards. One gallon is just 0.005 of a cubic yard."

6. "How many gallons are in one cubic yard?"

7. "One cubic yard of compost will fill how many 32-gallon bins full?"

Todd: "Rich organic soil allows farmers to grow food without artificial fertilizers. Last year, we kept 222,487 pounds of food waste out of the landfill!"

8. How many full tons did Todd and Jamie keep out of the landfill?

16

Gordon Ringberg

TALL SHIPS CAPTAIN

How would you like to be a sea captain, navigating a three-masted schooner from island to island for days and weeks, carried along by the wind in your sails?

Captain Ringberg does just that aboard both the two-masted schooner *Abbey Road* and the three-masted schooner *Zeeto*. As executive director of Lake Superior Tall Ships, Captain Ringberg's job is to deliver exciting, life-changing sailing adventures to adults, families, and youth groups.

Is there math involved? You bet.

"We do all sorts of math all the time. A lot of it is just in our heads. We often use distance equals speed times time." (d = s * t)

"It's 11:30 a.m. now, and we've just set sail on the *Zeeto* toward Cat Island, part of the Apostle Islands. Cat Island is 18 nautical miles from here, and the wind is enabling us to keep a steady pace of six knots. Knots is another word for nautical miles per hour."

DOI: 10.4324/9781003397700-16

1. Challenge: "What time can we expect to arrive?"

"When we're thinking about minutes instead of hours, we use
60 * d = s * t. In fact, the wind is picking up. I'd better check our speed."

2. Challenge: "In the last 20 minutes, we've traveled 2½ nautical miles. How fast did we travel in nautical miles per hour (knots)?"

"The more square feet of sail, the more wind power you have. Our two-masted schooner *Abbey Road* has 2,400 square feet of sail. *Zeeto*, our three-masted schooner, has 1,375 square feet of sail."

3. "How many times more sail power does *Abbey Road* have than *Zeeto*?" *(Round to the nearest hundredth.)*

"Sail area is not the only performance indicator. A sailboat that sits high in the water with a lot of sail will be more lively, but the ride will be rockier, bumpier."

"You can get an idea of the maximum speed a sailboat can go in a strong wind by looking at the water line length. The longer the water line, the faster a boat can go. From bow tip to stern, the *Abbey Road* is 57 feet long, but its water line length is just 41 feet. The *Zeeto* tip to stern is 65 feet, with a water line length of 44 feet."

4. "Which boat could theoretically go faster?"

"There have been occasional times like today when the wind died down to nothing, and we had no choice but to use our motor."

5. "If we motored 33 nautical miles around the islands at normal cruising speed of six knots, how long did we use the motor?"

"*Abbey Road* burns 1½ gallons an hour at normal cruising speed."

6. Challenge: "How much fuel did we use?"

"A lot of the math we do is in navigation. True north is the north pole. But a compass reads magnetic north, which can be far from true north. And magnetic north moves around every year! Plus, steel on the boat affects the compass reading. Math is real important if you want to get where you're going on a boat!"

"Uh, oh! The radio is warning of a violent storm by nightfall! We have to find a safe anchorage and get to shore. Really pushing at top speed, this boat burns 15 gallons an hour."

7. **Challenge: "A gallon of fuel lasts how many minutes at top speed?"**

8. **Challenge: "We started with a full 50-gallon tank of fuel from our harbor in Bayfield. At top speed, we're just two hours away. Can we make it back on the fuel we have?"**
(You'll need to use your answer from problem 6, and show your work.)

Why sail a tall ship?

"We know that bringing a tall ship to Lake Superior will not cure cancer, feed the hungry, or house the homeless. But our hope is that kids who sail with us will be inspired to do great things in the future, because they were able to see the world and themselves a little differently from the deck of a schooner."

[Captain Ringberg is also mayor of Bayfield, Wisconsin.]

17

Michael Pully

GUITAR SHOP OWNER

Michael Pully is living his passion. His first guitar shop was in the furnace room of his house. But so many people brought him guitars to fix that he had to expand into a bedroom. Then more and more people kept coming, so he opened his own shop—the Cozy Corner Guitar Shop. "There's math all over the place here," states Michael.

"Fender and Gibson are top names in electric guitars, but they're expensive, so people come to me to build one for them with the same specifications."

"To build guitars from scratch, you have to be able to add fractions and to convert fractions to decimals."

"To build a Fender Electric Stratocaster guitar, I get a solid slab of alder wood 15 inches wide, 18 inches long and 2 inches thick. Then I plane that down to 1¾ inches thick."

1. "How much did I take off the thickness of the wood?"

"Then I cut the wood to the right shape and sand it smooth."

"Next, I use a router tool to create cavities inside the guitar to hide the wiring. You have to be able to know what depth to go in from the top and from the bottom without cutting right through."

Copyright material from Marya Washington Tyler (2026), *Real World Math*, Routledge

DOI: 10.4324/9781003397700-17

43

"What would happen if we have a 1¾ inch body and we cut a ¾ inch deep cavity for electronics from one side, and on the other side we cut a cavity ½ inch deep?"

2. **Challenge: "How much does that leave us between the two?"**

"We always have to make sure we have enough space in between. If you don't, you're going to get a hole and it's ruined."

"I measure at least twice before I cut. Some of this wood is very expensive."

"Guitar strings vibrate when you play them, and you have to make sure you leave enough distance for the strings to vibrate. That's called the playing action. If you have a 0.046 inch string, it will triple in size, so it needs triple the space."

3. **"What is the playing action needed for a 0.046 string?"**

"Scale lengths are what really determines how the guitar sounds. To find scale length, you measure from the top nut to the 12th fret. Then you double that."

Model of guitar	Measure from top to 12th fret	Scale length
Paul Reed Smith	12½ inches	**4.**
Fender Electric	12¾ inches	**5.**
Gibson	12.375 inches	**6.**

"Most rulers don't show inches in decimal form. They show inches in fractions—eighths and sixteenths."

7. "How would ⅛ of an inch be written as a decimal?"

8. "What would the answer to question 6 be written as a fraction?"

"There's math everywhere here. Music is all math. Plus, I'm ordering lots of inventory, keeping track of how much money I'm taking in, putting some away for taxes, writing invoices, charging sales tax, working to maintain a profit margin of 40 points (which is how in business they say 40 percent).

9. "With a 40-point profit margin, what is my profit on $800?"

"It's fun to make money doing what you love."

18

Lu Salawater

Bad River Band of Lake Superior Chippewa

TRIBAL PROSECUTOR

"As Tribal Prosecutor, I argue in court the case against someone suspected of illegal activity. Then I use math to figure out the cost of damages to be paid."

"I also use math on the powwow planning committee. At powwows, there is drumming and singing in the Ojibwe language, and native dancing. We serve a variety of foods including manoomin ('wild rice'). Manoomin grows on our waters and is sacred in our culture."

"We're planning for 500 people to each eat ½ cup of rice. Manoomin expands as it cooks in water. One cup of uncooked rice becomes 3½ cups cooked."

1. **"How many cups of cooked rice do we need?"**

2. **Challenge: "How many whole cups of uncooked rice will we need?"** *(When rounding, consider that it's sometimes better to have a little extra than not enough.)*

"Since the powwow is free and open to the public, the Powwow Committee sells t-shirts to cover the costs. We ordered 200 t-shirts at $8 each, and sold them for $25 each. We were able to sell all but 6 t-shirts."

3. **"What was our total profit on tshirts?"**

DOI: 10.4324/9781003397700-18

"Many tribal members wear native regalia to the powwow. I'm making a 16-inch necklace using 8-millimeter round glass beads. I know there are about 25 millimeters in an inch."

4. "About how many millimeters long will the necklace be?"

5. "How many beads do I need?"

"Many of the women make and wear jingle dresses. The hem of the dress I am making is 57 inches around, and I want to attach jingle beads every 1½ inch."

6. "How many jingle beads will I need for the hem?"

"This year I am entering the Powwow Canoe Race. I'll have to paddle up the river against the current for 2 miles. The fastest time last year was 36 minutes."

7. "How long did it take them to paddle 1 mile?"

8. "How many miles/hour did they go?"

"It may not seem like the canoe was going very fast, but paddling against a current isn't easy! On the day of the race, the Bad River was flowing at 0.92 feet per second against them."

9. "How many feet per minute was the force of the current pushing against them?"

19

Mark Vinson, Ph.D.

FISHERIES SCIENTIST

We're aboard the research vessel *KIYI* (*kai ai*) on Lake Superior. Lake Superior is the largest freshwater lake in the world by surface area, and contains 10% of the world's freshwater. Meet Dr. Mark Vinson, Fisheries Scientist for the Great Lakes Science Center.

Mark likes his job.

"I love numbers. And I like fish and I like water. So here I am working with those three things—fish, water, and math."

"Pretty much everything you can think about a fish we have numbers for. We count them and weigh them and take parts off them, and from those parts we get different numbers: 'What did they eat?' … 'How many things did they eat?' … 'How old are they?'

"We measure how old a fish is by looking at the rings, just like tree rings, that form in a bone in its ear. The more rings, the older the fish."

The crew throws a trawl net off the stern of the boat, and the *KIYI* travels forward at 4 km per hour for 30 minutes, with the net dragging behind.

1. **How far did the net travel in kilometers?**

2. **How far did the net travel in meters?**

DOI: 10.4324/9781003397700-19

The net is 9 meters wide and will drag on the lake bottom, catching whatever is in its way.

3. Calculate the area of lake floor swept by the net.

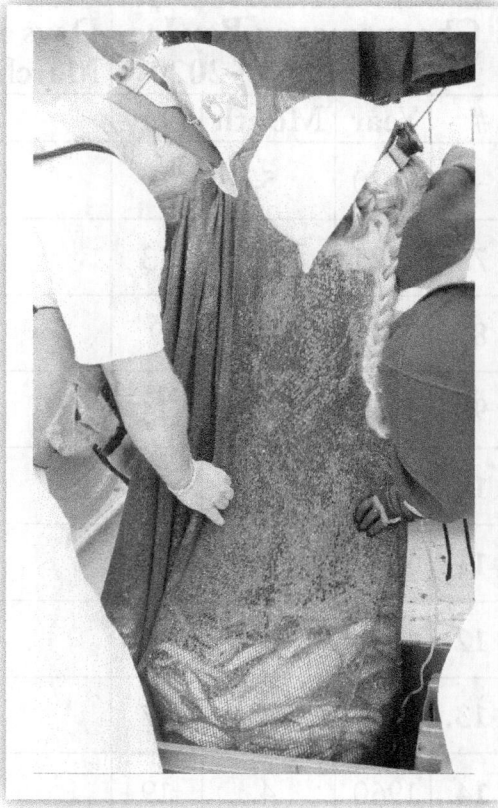

Scientists measure area in hectares. One hectare contains 10,000 square meters.

4. How many hectares did the net sweep?

The crew hauls the heavy net back onto the boat. The net is packed with big and little flipfloppy, squirmy fish. Quickly, the fish are sorted into species, counted, weighed, measured, and then dissected for further study. 530 fish were pulled in.

5. How many fish per hectare were caught?
(Round to nearest whole fish.)

The total weight of the fish caught was 4.5 kg.

6. What was the average weight of the fish caught? *(Round to nearest tenth of a gram.)*

"I check three places. I compare the numbers from different years, and I begin to see a trend."

"The *KIYI* travels around Lake Superior two or three times a year. We are going almost constantly when the water is not frozen. Knowing the date the ice breaks up every year can give us some valuable indications for the future."

Chequamegon Bay Ice Breakup 1920–2020				Days after March 31
#	Year	Month	Day	32
--	1920	5	2	
7.	1925	4	13	
8.	1930	4	9	
9.	1935	4	14	
10.	1940	4	28	
11.	1945	3	28	
12.	1950	5	2	
13.	1955	4	17	
14.	1960	4	19	
15.	1965	4	29	
16.	1970	4	11	
17.	1975	4	29	
18.	1980	4	24	
19.	1985	4	20	
20.	1990	4	18	
21.	1995	4	25	
22.	2000	3	26	
23.	2005	4	16	
24.	2010	4	2	
25.	2015	4	12	
26.	2020	4	9	

"Fill out the chart using negative numbers when necessary."

27. "Let's see if we can detect a trend. Using this data, find the average number of days after March 31, 1920 through 1940 that the ice breakup occurred." *(Find to the nearest tenth.)*

28. "Now find the average number of days after March 31, 2000 through 2020 that ice breakup occurred." *(Find to the nearest tenth.)*

29. "Does the ice appear to be breaking up sooner or later?"

"It is estimated that Lake Superior contains 3 quadrillion gallons of water. (That's 3 with 15 zeros after it.) It is also estimated that there are 2.2 billion fish in Lake Superior."

30. Challenge: "If all those fish were evenly spread across the whole of Lake Superior, how much water would each fish have to itself?" *(Round to the nearest tenth of a million gallons.)*

"I really just like numbers. I keep track of numbers of everything. How many hay bales came off my field. How many gallons of apple cider I made this year. My whole life is wrapped up in numbers."

"For us, there is a lot of math in knowing where you are on the lake. You can't say, 'We're by the big tree a little bit north of Bayfield.' In the past, 30 years ago, you would do that all on paper. Now it's all done with GPS. We're so reliant on electronics, if the GPS is not working, we go home. And hopefully it's not foggy, so we can find our way home."

"I find magic in the numbers. There are always patterns and trends. So it's a puzzle. It's a riddle. What are those numbers trying to tell me?"

20

Phoenix

GROCERY STORE ACCOUNTANT

"I enjoy doing math. Growing up in San Diego, my friend Ben and I would do math while we waited for the city bus. We'd look at the bus numbers listed on the board and, using math, try to make one of the other bus numbers."

"So let's say there was Bus 24, Bus 36, and Bus 60. We'd think about it for a while, and then I'd yell, '24 plus 36 is 60!' Or Ben would shout, '60 minus 36 is 24!' And whoever was first would win. Sometimes I won. Sometimes Ben."

"So the rule is to use every single bus number once. You can use addition, subtraction, multiplication, and division to solve, and the solution has to be one of the bus numbers."

"Here's an example."

BUS 12	BUS 14	BUS 84	BUS 33	BUS 9

1. "Can I make 84 by adding together the other numbers?"

2. "What if I do 14 – 12 and multiply that times 33 + 9? Does that make 84?"

3. "Fill in the blanks to write that as an equation."

   (   ) (   ) = 84

Copyright material from Marya Washington Tyler (2026), *Real World Math*, Routledge

DOI: 10.4324/9781003397700-20

4. **"Now try to use the other numbers to make 9. Write the equation."**

$$84 \div (\qquad -12) - \qquad = 9$$

"You can play a really fun game like our bus game, but easier, with other kids standing in a circle around a table, using a deck of cards. Take the face cards out. You won't need them. Ace counts as 1. Now choose a number you're all going to try to make. Let's start with 24, because 24 has a lot of factors: 1, 2, 3, 4, 6, 8, 12, 24."

"Now put any four cards face up on the table and see who can use them to make 24 first. You can add, subtract, multiply, or divide, but use each card only once. When you find a way to make 24, you quick slap your hand on the table nice and loud, and then explain to the group how you figured it out. If you're right, you keep those cards."

5. **"Got it? Let's pretend these four cards are on the table. Find a way to make 24 using each card once. There may be more than one way."** *(Your answer will need to be written as an equation for this book.)*

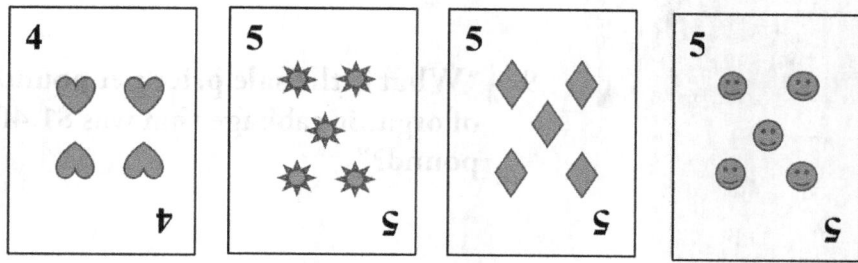

"If nobody in your group could find a way to make 24 with those cards, you could put out another card. And you can keep putting out cards if you need to, but usually you don't need more than four cards."

6. **"Now try this one. You can do it!"** *(Write your answer as an equation.)*

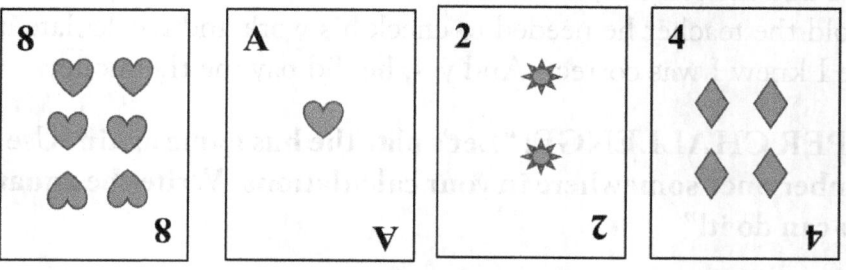

"Math has really helped me at my job. I started in the deli department, because I like cooking. But I was offered this position because I have taken lots of math, and I like it! Plus it pays more."

"Whenever something goes on sale, it's my job to calculate the new price. If the calculation is an easy one, like today's 10% off sale, I just do it in my head."

7. "What is the sale price of a box of Cocoa Crispies™ cereal that was $4.00?"

8. "What is the sale price of a can of ravioli that was $3.50?"

9. "What is the sale price per pound of organic cabbage that was $1.40 a pound?"

"When I was in sixth grade, the teacher offered each person in the class $100 if we would get every problem on a test right. There were a whole lot of really tough problems. I worked very hard to get every one right. When he handed back my paper after checking it, he told me, 'Sorry.' I had missed one, he said."

"I told the teacher he needed to check his work and recalculate it, because I knew I was correct. And yes, he did pay me the money."

10. SUPER CHALLENGE: "Let's play the bus game again. Use each number once somewhere in your calculations. Write the equation. You can do it!"

BUS 12	BUS 14	BUS 18	BUS 20	BUS 9	BUS 4

ANSWER KEY

1

Kealy White

BAKERY MANAGER

1. How many times larger is the sheet pan than the small batch pan?
   9 x 13 = 117 square inches   26 x 18 = 468 square inches
   468 ÷ 117 = **4 times larger**

	Ingredients	Amount 1 batch	Amount 16 batches	
			# grams	**# kg**
2.	1¼ cup dark chocolate chips	215 grams	**3,440 g**	**3.4 kg**
3.	1½ cups garbanzo beans	250 grams	**4,000 g**	**4 kg**
4.	2 eggs	2 eggs	**32 eggs**	—
5.	2 tablespoons cocoa powder	14.76 grams	**236.16 g**	—
6.	¼ teaspoon cinnamon	0.7 grams	**11.2 g**	—
7.	1 tablespoon coconut oil	13.6 grams	**217.6 g**	—
8.	2 teaspoons vanilla extract	4.2 grams	**67.2 g**	—
9.	⅓ cup coconut sugar	60 grams	**960 g**	—
10.	½ teaspoon of baking powder	2.5 grams	**40 g**	—
11.	½ teaspoon salt	3.5 grams	**56 g**	—
12.	½ cup confectioner's sugar	62 grams	**992 g**	—

13. What's the average of the two temperatures?
    350 + 325 = 675
    675 ÷ 2 = **337.5 degrees F**

14. Challenge: If each brownie is cut 3″ wide, how long will each one be?
    18″ wide with each 3″ wide = 6 rows of brownies
    48 brownies total wanted / 6 rows = 8 columns of brownies
    Pan 26″ ÷ 8 columns = **3.25 inches each**

26"

18"

2
Joy Ratkowski
HORSE THERAPIST

1. How many times are the horses' hooves trimmed per year?
   (52 weeks)
   52 weeks ÷ 4 = **13 times a year**

2. How much does hoof trimming cost us per year?
   13 • $40 each = $520 per horse/year
   $520 • 22 horses = **$11,440 total**

3. Our 22 horses drink how many gallons per year? *(365 days = 1 year)*
   22 horses • 10 gallons/day = 220 gallons/day
   220 • 365 days/year = **80,300 gallons/year**

4. About how much hay should we give each horse daily?
   2.5% = 0.025
   0.025 • 1000 = **25 pounds**

5. About how many pounds of hay should we give out each day?
   25 • 22 = **550 pounds**

6. About how many pounds of hay will we need for one year?
   (365 days)
   550 • 365 = **200,750 pounds**

7. How many bales do I need to order? *(Round up to the nearest whole bale.)*
   200,750 pounds ÷ 1000 = 200.750 pounds
   200.75 bales rounds up to **201 bales**

8. How much will we spend on hay this year?
   250 • 100 = 25,000
   375 • 50 = 18,750

   $25,000 for grass bales
   +$18,750 for alfalfa bales
   $43,750

9. Challenge: How much does Dolly weigh to the nearest pound?

$$\frac{(\textit{Heart girth in inches} \cdot \textit{heart girth in inches}) \cdot \textit{body length}}{330} = \textit{weight in pounds}$$

$$\frac{(69 \cdot 69) \cdot 70}{330} = 1,009.9$$

1,009.9 rounded to the nearest pound = **1,010 pounds**

10. Clydesdale horse	**17 hands**	68 inches
11. Shetland pony	9 hands 2 inches	**38 inches**
12. Quarter horse	**15 hands**	60 inches
13. Arabian horse	14 hands 3 inches	**59 inches**

14. Is she overweight? *(Show your work.)*
    44 • 1.26 = 55.44
    13 • 4 = 52 inches 52 + 2 = 54 inches
    55.44 > 54 Yes, Penny is overweight.

15. How far is the distance around in feet? *(Round to the nearest foot.)*
    (Circumference equals pi times diameter, and pi = 3.14)
    C = 3.14 • 90 feet
    C = 282.6
    C = **283 feet**

16. How many galloping strides will a horse take in a full circle of the arena? *(Round to nearest whole stride.)*
    283 ÷ 4.5 = 62.9
    63 strides

3
Shane Peltonen
ADVENTURE TREKKER

1. The temperature dropped at least how many degrees overnight?
   60 − 32 = **28 degrees**

2. If it rained ½ inch of rain every day for 33 days, how much did it rain?

   $33 \bullet \dfrac{1}{2} = \dfrac{33}{2} = 33 \div 2 =$ **16½ inches**

3. How many ounces of water was I carrying?
   1 liter = 35.2 ounces
   8 liters = (35.2 ounces • 8 liters) = **281.6 ounces**

4. How many pounds of water was I carrying?
   281.6 ounces ÷ 16 ounces per pound = **17.6 pounds**

5. How many pounds of food do I need to carry for 15 days?
   15 days • 2 pounds per day = **30 pounds**

6. How many pounds of gear am I carrying?

my empty backpack:	2.0 pounds
my shelter: just a tarp and groundsheet	1.0 pound
extra clothing, hat, coat	2.0 pounds
water purification system	0.5 pounds
insect repellant, nail clippers, bandages, etc.	2.5 pounds
electrolyte packets, vitamins/minerals	0.5 pounds
phone, batteries, headlamp, satellite messenger	1.5 pounds
multitool, repair tape, scissors,	0.5 pound
	10.5 pounds

7. If I'm heading out with 8 liters of water and 15 days' food, how many total pounds will I be carrying?

water (8 liters)	17.6 pounds
food for 15 days	30.0 pounds
gear	10.5 pounds
total	**58.1 pounds**

8. Challenge: Will I make it over the mountains in time? *(Show your math.)*

2,400 miles total to go ÷ 23 per day = 104.3 days of hiking

> **31 days July**
> **31 days August**
> **30 days September**
> <u>**15 or 16 days October**</u>
> **107 or 108 days until snow**

Whew, I just might make it! **YES!**

9. When I finish, how many miles will I have hiked in all?
   1,000-mile Arizona Trail
      550-mile Superior Hiking Trail
   4,800-mile North Country Trail
   1,200-mile Ice Age Trail
      300-mile Long Trail
   3,200-mile Continental Divide Trail
      550-mile Colorado Trail
   2,650-mile Pacific Crest Trail
   6,800-mile American Discovery Trail
   <u>2,550 mile Pinhoti/Appalachian Trail</u>
   23,600 miles in all

   (Editor's note: the circumference of the Earth is 24,901 miles.)

4

Aquiles Garcia Cardoso

RESTAURANT OWNER

1. Subtracting this cost, how much money do we make?
$14.99 • 80 = 1,199.20 cash
1,199.20 − 800 = **$399.20 income**

2. How much money do we make?
$3.75 • 100 = $375
375 − 40 = **$345**

3. What do I have left?
345 − 80 − 50 =
or 345 − (80 + 50) =
345 − 130 = **$215**

4. How much do I make on each order of extra tomatoes?
5 − 2 = 3
$3 ÷ 5 = 3/5 = 0.6 = **$0.60**

5. How much does a starting chef get per overtime hour?

$1½ • 18 = \dfrac{3}{2} • 18 =$

$\dfrac{3}{2} • \dfrac{18}{1} =$ **$27 per hour for overtime**

6. Challenge: If a starting chef works 48 hours, what is his pay?
18 • 40 hours = $720 normal weekly pay
27 • 8 overtime hours worked = $216 overtime pay
720 + 216 = **$936**

5

Ted Gostomski

BIRD BIOLOGIST

1. What time do I want to arrive?
   Sunrise at 5:09 a.m. = 4:69
   4:69 − 30:00 = **4:39 a.m. arrive at listening point**

2. What time do I have to get up?
   20 min. get ready + 35 min. driving + 45 min. hiking = 100 minutes
   100 minutes = 1 hour 40 minutes = 1:40
   4:39 need to arrive − 1:40 =
   3:99 need to arrive − 1:40 = **2:59 a.m. time to get up!**

3. What time would I get home?
   Sunrise 5:09 + 4 hours = 9:09 a.m.
   9:09 + 45 min. hiking = 9:54 a.m.
   9:54 a.m. + 35 min. driving = 9:89 = **10:29 a.m.**

4. What is the ratio of frugivore species to omnivores?
   4 to 6 = **2 to 3 or 2:3 or 2/3**

5. Challenge:
   What is the difference in the slope of grassland birds and urban birds?
   8.00 − (− 0.26) = **8.26**

6. What percent of species are permanent residents all year?
   4 + 6 + 10 = 20 species
   10/20 = ½ = **50% permanent residents**

7. What percent migrate within the continental United States?
   4/20 = 20/100 = **20% migrate within US**

8. What percent migrate to the tropics?
   6/20 = 30/100 = **30% migrate to tropics**

6
Molly Lawton
ANIMAL SHELTER MANAGER

1. How many milliliters of dewormer do I give Snoopy? *Round to nearest tenth.*
    34.6 milliliters ÷ 10 pounds = 3.46 milliliters
    3.5 milliliters

2. How many ounces of water could I safely give Ralph?
    1 ounce of fluid / pound • 10 pounds = 10 ounces
    10 ounces

3. How many milliliters of water could I safely give Ralph?
    10 ounces • 30 milliliters = **300 milliliters of water**

4. 1 milliliter of Amoxicillin equals how many milligrams?
    5 milliliters = 400 milligrams
    400 ÷ 5 = 80 milligrams
    1 milliliter = **80 milligrams**

5. Challenge: Find the correct dosage to give the nearest tenth of a milliliter
    How many milliliters = 62.5 milligrams of Amoxicillin?
    What part of 80 is 62.5?
    See it as a fraction. 62.5/80
    62.5 milligrams ÷ 80 milligrams/milliliter
    62.5 milligrams ÷ 80 = 0.78 milliliters, so to be safe, **0.7 milliliters**

EASIER WAY TO SOLVE ANY COMPLICATED PROBLEM LIKE THIS: Create an equation using what you know, setting it up so that the answer you're looking for (millilliters) is in the numerator, and all the other words cancel out:

$$\frac{5 \text{ milliliters}}{400 \text{ milligrams}} \bullet \frac{62.5 \text{ milligrams}}{1} = \mathbf{\underline{0.78\ ml}, \text{ rounded}} \text{ to } \mathbf{0.7\ milliliters}$$

7
Nathan Mitchell
ORCHESTRA CONDUCTOR

1. The brass section is what fraction of the orchestra? *(Reduce the fraction.)*

   $\dfrac{11}{44} = \dfrac{1}{4}$ **of the orchestra**

2. The woodwind section is what fraction of the orchestra?

   $\dfrac{9}{44}$ **of the orchestra**

3. The string section is what fraction of the orchestra?

   $\dfrac{23}{44}$ **of the orchestra**

4. Is the string section more or less than half the orchestra?

   $\dfrac{23}{44}$ strings $> \dfrac{22}{44}$ half the orchestra

   More

5. A song written for 180 beats per minute means how many beats per second?
   180 beats/60 seconds =
   180÷60 = **3 beats/second**

6. If a song is written at 90 beats per minute. how many beats is that per second?
   90 beats / 60 seconds = 3/2

   $\dfrac{3}{2} = 1\dfrac{1}{2}$ **beats per second**

7. If a song is 90 beats per minute, how many beats is that every two seconds?
   1½ beat in one second
   3 beats every two seconds

8. 4 eighth-notes are how many total beats?
   One eighth note = ½ beat

   4 eighths notes = $4 \bullet \dfrac{1}{2} = \dfrac{4}{2}$ = **2 beats**

9. Challenge: How many sixteenth notes would fit in the rest of this measure?
4 beats total − 2 beats = 2 beats left
2 beats ÷ ¼ beat each = **8 sixteenth notes**

10. Movement I 486 seconds ÷ 60 = 8.1 **8 minutes**

11. Movement II 179 seconds ÷ 60 = 2.98 **3 minutes**

12. Movement III 481 seconds ÷ 60 = 8.01 **8 minutes**

13. Movement IV 993 seconds ÷ 60 = 16.55 **17 minutes**

8
Amaris
FOOD SHELF MANAGER

1. What percent of our donated food should go to the South Shore food shelf? *Round to the nearest whole percent.*
    24 South Shore households ÷ 450 total = 0.05333 = **5% of the food**

2. What percent of our donated food should Ashland get? *(Round to the nearest whole percent.)*
    278 in Ashland ÷ 450 total households = 0.61777 = **62% of the food**

3. Donation can be safely distributed until this date: Yogurt
    21 + 10 = 31, but there are only 30 days in April.
    May 1, 2026
    Received on April 12—**Y**

4. Donation can be safely distributed until this date: Cream cheese
    2 weeks = 14 days
    24 + 14 = 38
    38 days − 31 days in March = 7 days more
    April 7, 2026
    Received on April 12—**N**

5. Donation can be safely distributed until this date: Hard cheese
    6 months after October = **April 17, 2026**
    Received on April 12—**Y**

6. Donation can be safely distributed until this date: Soft cheese
    7 days + April 7 = **April 14, 2026**
    Received on April 12—**Y**

7. Donation can be safely distributed until this date: Eggs in shell
    31 days − 18 days = 13 days left in March
    4 weeks = 28 days
    28 − 13 = 15 days
    April 15, 2026
    Received on April 12—**Y**

8. Donation can be safely distributed until this date: Butter
April 28, 2025—N

			REFRIGERATED DONATIONS SAFETY CHECK		
#	Donation	Product can be safely consumed past:	"Best by" date we see on the label	Donation can be safely distributed until this date:	Keep? Y or N
3.	Yogurt	**10 days**	April 21, 2026	**May 1, 2026**	Y
4.	Cream cheese	**2 weeks**	March 24, 2026	**April 7, 2026**	N
5.	Hard cheese	**6 months**	October 17, 2025	**April 17, 2026**	Y
6.	Soft cheese	**1 week**	April 7, 2026	**April 14, 2026**	Y
7.	Eggs in shell	**4 weeks**	March 18, 2026	**April 15, 2026**	Y
8.	Butter	**2 months**	February 28, 2025	**April 28, 2025**	N

9. Calculate the average number of children per household. *Round to the nearest tenth.*

Month	Households	Children 0–17	**Adults 18-60**	**Adults over 60**	**Total People**
TOTAL	3,313	2,087	**3,921**	**2,002**	**8,011**

2,087 children ÷ 3,313 households = 0.6299 = **0.6 children**

9

Addie Arens

HEAD LIBRARIAN

1. What percent were HARDCOVER BOOKS? *(nearest whole percent.)*
   3,008 ÷ 4,599 = 0.654 = **65%**

2. What percent were OTHER BOOKS? *(nearest whole percent.)*
   403 ÷ 4,599 = 0.087 = **9%**

3. What percent were LARGE PRINT BOOKS? *(nearest whole percent.)*
   80 ÷ 4,599 = 0.017 =**2%**

4. Based on this information, how much should I spend on BOOKS?
   65% + 9% + 2% = 76%
   0.76 ● 6,500 = **$4,940**

5. Fill out the CHANGE column below with the amount of increase or decrease from the previous month.

PATRON COUNTS		CHANGE
January	578	**0**
February	580	**+2**
March	596	**+16**
April	595	**–1**
May	604	**+9**
June	607	**+3**
July	611	**+4**
August	613	**+2**
September	621	**+8**
October	623	**+2**
November	625	**+2**
December	627	**+2**
TOTAL	7280	**+49**

6. What was the total change? (indicate plus or minus) **+49**

7. What was the average monthly change? (Round to the nearest whole percent)
   49 ÷ 12 = + 4.08
   + 4%

10
Anne Workman
STATE TROOPER

1. How fast did I have to drive to catch this speeder?

> PROBLEM SOLVING STRATEGY:
> Set up the problem to cancel out the words that
> you don't want, leaving just the answer.
>
> $$\frac{1.5 \text{ miles}}{1 \text{ minute}} \cdot \frac{60 \text{ minute}}{\text{hour}} = \frac{90 \text{ miles}}{\text{hour}}$$

Or:

3/2 miles/1 minute • 60 minutes/hour = 180/2 = **90 miles per hour**

2. Challenge: How fast was this person going?
   4 miles/3 minutes • 60 minutes/hour = 240/3 = **80 miles/hour**

Note to teacher: Problems 4–6 provide opportunity for discussion on rounding, where to round, when to round, and to what place, and the effects of each.

Find each one's speed to the nearest tenth of a mph, and record the number of miles over the speed limit.

3. 4 miles/3.2 minutes = 1.25 miles/minute
   1.25 miles/minute • 60 minutes/hour = **75 miles per hour**
   75 − 55 = **20 mph over speed limit**

4. 4 miles/3.6 minutes = 1.11 miles/minute
   1.11 miles/minute • 60 minutes/hour =
   66.7 mph (*or* **66.6** *or* **66** *or* **67** *based on where student rounded*)
   66.7 − 55 = **11.7** (*or* **11.6** *or* **11** *or* **12**) **mph over speed limit**

5. 4 miles/3.4 minutes = 1.18 miles/minute
   1.18 miles/minute • 60 minutes/hour =
   70.8 miles per hour (*or* **70.6** *or* **71** *or* **72** mph *due to rounding variations*)
   70.8 − 55 = **15.6 mph over speed limit** (*or* **15.8** *or* **16** *or* **17** *based on rounding*)

6.   4 miles/2.9 minutes = 1.38 miles/minute

1.38 miles/minute • 60 minutes/hour = **82.8 miles per hour (*or* 83 *or* 84)**

82.8 − 55 = **27.8 mph over speed limit (*or* 28 *or* 29 *based on where student rounded*)**

11
Petty Officer Malcolm Venus
SEARCH AND RESCUER

1. If you know distance and time, how can you find speed?
   speed = distance / time
   or
   speed = distance ÷ time

2. If you know speed and distance, how can you find time?
   time = distance / speed
   or
   time = distance ÷ speed

3. 960 yards is how far in nautical miles? *(Round to nearest tenth.)*
   960/2000 = 0.48 nautical miles = **0.5 nautical miles**

4. How long have we been searching? *(Give the answer in decimal hours.)*
   1 min. + 1 min. + 2 min. + 2 min. + 3 min. + 3 min. = 12 minutes
   12/60 = **0.2 hours**

5. How fast is the life ring drifting in nautical miles/hour?
   When we see the symbol / (as in NM/hr), we know to divide the top number by the bottom number.
   0.5 nautical miles / 0.2 hours = **2.5 nautical miles/hour**

6. 1 NM = 1 knot
   How fast is the life ring drifting in knots
   2.5 knots

7. How many nautical miles did we travel?
   10,000 yards / 2,000 = **5 NM**

8. Challenge: How many minutes did it take us to get there?
   5 NM / 25 knots = 5 NM ÷ 25 knots = 0.2 hours
   0.2 hours • 60 = 12 minutes

9. How fast did our boat travel back to base?
15 NM / 0.5 hours = 30 nautical miles/hour = **30 knots**

10. If we received the distress call at 1230 and the mission was completed in an hour and a half, what time did we finish?
1230 + 130 = **1400**

12
Abby Klema
ALPACA FARMER

1. How many pounds of hay can Frank eat per day?
   150 pounds • 0.015 pounds/day = **2.25 pounds/day**

2. How many pounds of hay can he eat per week?
   2.25 pounds/day • 7 days/week = **15.75 or 15¾ pounds/week**

3. Challenge: About how many bales will Frank eat in a week?
   (*Give answer as a fraction.*)
   15.75 ÷ 60 = 0.2625 = **about ¼ of a bale**

4. How much does baby Bell weigh?
   207.4 pounds − (178 pounds + 0.6 pounds) =
   207.4 pounds − 178.6 pounds = **28.8 pounds**

5. Has she doubled her weight?
   14 pounds • 2 = 28 pounds (healthy weight)
   28.8 Mozzarella's weight > 28 pounds **Yes!**

6. How many pounds of fleece can we expect from our 27 alpacas?
   6.5 • 27 = **175.5 pounds of fleece**

7. How many pounds of prime fleece will we get?
   175.5 ÷ 2 = **87.75 pounds of prime fleece**

8. How many pairs of socks can we expect?
   87.75 ÷ 0.4 = 219.375 (but nobody wants 0.375 of a pair of socks)
   219 pairs of socks

13

Ben Connors

TRIBAL PLANNER

1. How many cubic feet of gravel do I need per mile?
    5,280 feet • 22 feet • 0.5 feet = **58,080 cubic feet**

2. How many cubic yards is that? *(round to the nearest yard)*
    1 cubic yard = 3 feet • 3 feet • 3 feet = 27 cubic feet
    58,080 cubic feet ÷ 27 cu.ft./cu.yd. = 2,151.11 = **2,151 cubic yards**

3. How many whole tons should I order?
    1 cubic yard = 1.25 tons
    2,151 cubic yards • 1.25 tons/cubic yard = 2,688.75 tons
    2,689 tons

14
Rachel Frydenlund
SKI RACE COORDINATOR

1. How many degrees below freezing was it?
   $32° - (-13°) = 32° + 13° =$ **45° F below freezing**

2. How many ounces of drink will we need?
   10,000 racers • 7 ounces drink = 70,000 ounces needed

3. How many gallons should I order?
   70,000 ounces ÷ 128 ounces/gallon = 546.875 gallons = **547 gallons**

4. How many 5-gallon buckets do I need? *(Make sure your answer makes sense.)*
   547 gallons ÷ 5 = 109.4 buckets, so I need to get **110 five-gallon buckets**

5. How many tubes for each bucket?
   36 tablets ÷ 12 tablets/tube = **3 tubes/bucket**

6. How many tubes do I need to order? *(Round up to the nearest ten tubes.)*
   109.4 five-gallon buckets • 3 tubes/ bucket = 328.2 tubes = **330 tubes**

7. Which aid stations are the farthest apart?

29.5 K Gravel Pit	50.0 K Finish Line
−20.6 K Double 0	41.1 K Fish Hatchery
8.9 kilometers	8.9 kilometers

   Two are tied. Double 0 to Gravel Pit and Fish Hatchery to Finish Line.

8. How much faster was 2023 than 1973?

2 hours	48 minutes	16.00 seconds =	2 hrs	47 min	76.00 sec
− 2 hours	5 minutes	39.93 seconds =	−2 hrs	5 min	39.93 sec
				42 minutes	36.07 seconds

9. How many pounds am I planning per racer?
16 ounces = 1 pound **1½ pounds**

10. How many pounds of soup should I order?
1½ pounds ● 10,000 racers = **15,000 pounds of soup**

11. How many full cases of soup should I order?
One case of soup = four 4-pound bags = 16 pounds/case
15,000 pounds ÷ 16 pounds/case = 937.5 cases
Because you can't order part of a case = **938 cases**

15
Jamie Tucker and Todd Rothe
ORGANIC COMPOSTERS

1. How much does she pay for us to pick up her food scraps every month?
    $30 first bin + $20 second bin = $50
    50 +15% of 50 =
    50 + 0.15 • 50 =
    50 + 7.50 =
    $57.50 per month

2. Combined, how much waste did her two bins contain?
    64.8 + 72.9 =137.7 weight of Mildred's two bins
    20.4 • 2 = 40.8 weight of two empty bins
    137.7 − 40.8 = **96.9 pounds of waste**

3. How much green waste did we add?
    2,020.4 − 638.5 = **1,381.9 pounds of green waste**

4. How many cubic-foot bags can we fill from one cubic yard of compost?
    One cubic yard = 3 feet by 3 feet by 3 feet
    3 • 3 • 3 = **27 bags**

5. How heavy is a one-cubic-foot bag of compost? (*to the nearest pound*)?
    1,000 pounds ÷ 27 bags/cubic yard = **37 pounds**

6. One cubic yard equals how many gallons?
    1 cu.yd. ÷ 0.005 cu.yd./gal. = **200 gallons**

7. One cubic yard of compost will fill how many 32-gallon bins?
    200 gallons/cubic yard ÷ 32 gallons/bin = 6.25 bins = **6 full bins**

8. How many full tons did Todd and Jamie keep out of the landfill?
    222,487 pounds ÷ 2,000 pounds/ton = 111.2435 tons = **111 tons**

16

Gordon Ringberg
TALL SHIPS CAPTAIN

1. Challenge: What time can we expect to arrive?
   (Remember: d = s • t)
   18 nautical miles = 6 nautical miles/hour • time
   18 / 6 = t
   Time = 3 hours
   11:30 + 3 = **14:30 nautical time**
   or
   14:30 – 12 = **2:30 p.m.**

2. Challenge: I know we've traveled 2½ nautical miles in the last 20 minutes, so how fast did we travel?
   60 • d = s • t
   60 • 2.5 = s • 20
   150 = s • 20
   150 ÷ 20 = s
   s = 7.5 knots

3. How many times more sail power does *Abbey Road* have than *Zeeto*?
   (Round to the nearest hundredth.)
   2,400 ÷ 1,375 = 1.74545454 ≅ **1.75 times more power**

4. Which boat could theoretically go faster?
   The *Zeeto*.

5. How long have we been using the motor?
   33 nautical miles / 6 nautical miles/hr = $5\frac{3}{6}$
   5½ hours (or 5 hours and 30 minutes)

6. Challenge: How much fuel have we used?
   1½ gallons/hour • 5½ hours =
   3/2 • 11/2 = 33/4 gallons
   33/4 = 8¼ gallons

7. Challenge: A gallon of fuel lasts how many minutes at top speed?
   15 gallons per hour
   1 gallon lasts 1/15 hour
   1/15 • 60 minutes = **4 minutes**

8. Challenge: We started with a full 50-gallon tank of fuel. We're just two hours at top speed from our harbor in Bayfield. Can we make it back on the fuel we have? *(Show your work.)*

50 gallons − 8 ¼ gallons = 41 ¾ gallons left before the storm

15 gallons/hour • 2 hours back = 30 gallons used at top speed

41 ¾ gallons − 30 gallons = 11 ¾ gallons left

YES!

17

Michael Pully

GUITAR SHOP OWNER

1. How much did I take off the thickness of the wood?

$$2 - 1\frac{3}{4} = \frac{1}{4}\text{ inch}$$

2. Challenge: How much does that leave us between the two?

$$1\frac{3}{4} - \left(\frac{3}{4} + \frac{1}{2}\right) \qquad = 1\frac{3}{4} - \left(\frac{3}{4} + \frac{2}{4}\right) = \qquad 1\frac{3}{4} - \left(\frac{5}{4}\right) \quad =$$

$$1\frac{3}{4} - 1\frac{1}{4} = \qquad \frac{2}{4} \qquad = \qquad \frac{1}{2}\text{ inch}$$

3. What is the playing action needed for a 0.046 string?
   0.046 • 3 = **0.138 inch**

Model of Guitar	Measure from top to 12th fret	Scale Length (multiply times 3)
Paul Reed Smith	12½ inches	**4. 25 inch**
Fender Electric	12¾ inches	**5. 25½ inch**
Gibson	12.375 inches	**6. 24.75 inch**

7. How would 1/8 of an inch be written as a decimal?
   1 ÷ 8 = **0.125 inch**

8. What would the answer to question 6 be when written as a fraction?

   $$24.75 = 24\,\frac{75}{1000} = \textbf{24¾ inches}$$

9. With a 40-point profit margin, what is my profit on $800?
   800 • 0.40 = **$320**

18
Lu Salawater
TRIBAL PROSECUTOR

1. How many cups of cooked rice do we need?
   500 people • ½ cup each = 500 ÷ 2 = **250 cups cooked rice**

2. Challenge: How many cups of uncooked rice will we need?
   1 cup uncooked = 3.5 cups cooked
   250 cups cooked ÷ 3.5 cups cooked
   250 ÷ 3.5 = 71.42 cups = **72 cups**

3. What was our total profit on t-shirts?
   200 t-shirts • $8 each = $1,0 spent
   200 t-shirts – 6 = 194 t-shirts sold
   194 t-shirts • $25 each = $4850.00 brought in
   $4,850 brought in – $1600 spent = **$3250.00 profit**

4. About how many millimeters long will the necklace be?
   16 in • 25 mm/in = **400 millimeters**

5. How many beads do I need?
   400 mm ÷ 8 mm beads = **50 beads**

6. How many jingle beads will I need for the hem?
   57 inches ÷ 1½ apart =
   57 ÷ 3/2 =
   57 • 2/3 = 114/3
   114/3 = **38 beads**

7. How long did it take for them to paddle 1 mile?
   2 miles in 36 minutes
   1 mile in **18 minutes**

8. How many miles per hour did the canoe travel?
   How many miles in 60 minutes?
   1 mile in 18 minutes
   60 ÷ 18 = 3⅓ miles per hour or 3.3 miles per hour

9. How many feet/minute was the force of the current pushing against them?
   0.92 feet • 60 seconds/minute = **55.2 feet every minute**

19
Mark Vinson, Ph.D.
FISHERIES SCIENTIST

1. How far did the net travel in kilometers? **2 km**

2. How far did the net travel in meters? **2,000 meters**

3. Calculate the area of lake floor swept by the net.
   2,000 meters • 9 meters = **18,000 square meters**

4. How many hectares did the net sweep?
   18,000 square meters ÷ 10,000 square meters = **1.8 hectares**

5. How many fish per hectare were caught? *(Round to the nearest whole fish.)*
   530 ÷ 1.8 = 294.444
   294 fish

6. What was the average weight? *(Round to the nearest tenth of a gram.)*
   4.5 kg = 4,500 grams
   4,500 grams ÷ 530 = 8.490566
   8.5 grams

#	Year	Month	Day	Days after March 31
Chequamegon Bay Ice Breakup 1920-2020				
	1920	5	2	32
7.	1925	4	13	13
8.	1930	4	9	9
9.	1935	4	14	14
10.	1940	4	28	28
11.	1945	3	28	-3
12.	1950	5	2	32
13.	1955	4	17	17
14.	1960	4	19	19
15.	1965	4	29	29
16.	1970	4	11	11

17.	1975	4	29	**29**
18.	1980	4	24	**24**
19.	1985	4	20	**20**
20.	1990	4	18	**18**
21.	1995	4	25	**25**
22.	2000	3	26	**-5**
23.	2005	4	16	**16**
24.	2010	4	2	**2**
25.	2015	4	12	**12**
26.	2020	4	9	**9**

27. Find the average days after for the years 1920 through 1940.
32 + 13 + 9 + 14 + 28 = 96
96 ÷ 5 = **19.2 days average**

28. Find the average days after for the years 2000 through 2020.
−5 + 16 + 2 + 12 + 9 = 34
34 ÷ 5 = **6.8 days average**

29. Does the ice appear to be breaking up sooner or later? **Sooner**

30. Challenge: How much water would each fish have to itself? *(Round to the nearest tenth of a million gallons.)*
3 quadrillion gallons: 3,000,000,000,000,000 gallons
2 billion looks like this: 2,000,000,000
So 2.2 billion looks like this 2,200,000,000
3,000,000,000,000,000 ÷ 2,200,000,000 =
3,000,000,0~~00,000,000~~ ÷ 2,2~~00,000,000~~ =
30,000,000 ÷ 22 = 1,363,636.36 gallons
Each fish would have 1.4 million gallons of water for itself.

20
Phoenix

GROCERY STORE ACCOUNTANT

1. Can I make 84 by adding together the other numbers? **NO**

2. What if I do 14–12 and multiply that times 33+9? Does that make 84? **YES**

3. Fill in the blanks to write that as an equation.
   (14 – 12) (33 + 9) = 84

4. Now try to use the other numbers to make 9. Write the equation.
   84 ÷ **(14 –12) – 33** = 9

5. Make 24 using cards 4 5 5 5 *(Write your answer as an equation.)*
   Example: (5 • 5) – (5 – 4) = 24

6. Make 24 using cards 8 A 2 4 *(Write your answer as an equation.)*
   Example:
   (8 + 4) (2) (1) = 24
   or
   (8 – 2) • (4) • (1) = 24
   or
   8 • (4 – 2 + 1) = 24
   or
   8 • [4 – (2 – 1)] = 24

7. 0.10 • 4.00 = 0.40
   4.00 – 0.40 = **$3.60**
   or
   0.90 • 4.00 = **$3.60**

8. 0.10 • 3.50 = 0.35
   3.50 – 0.35 = **$3.15**

9. 0.10 • 1.40 = 0.14
   1.40 – 0.14 = **$1.26/pound**

10. Super Challenge:
    Use each number once to make an equation: 12 14 84 33 9
    Example: (14–12) (20–18) (9-4) = 20

Math Field Trips? Why Not!

Protein Grocery Store Scavenger Hunt: Head to the grocery store for a fun field trip. Imagine you're heading out on a cross-country trek, and you're looking for the lightest weight food you can find. Which team can find the lightest gram of protein? Practice doing the math looking at various nutrition labels, and then, in groups of two, head to the grocery store with calculators, pens, and notepads. Compare your findings back at school. **Tip:** Call to let the grocery store staff know you're coming first. Stick with the grocery section, and exclude all refrigerated and frozen items. Remember to thank the manager and give the customers plenty of room to shop.

Cheapest Calorie Grocery Store Scavenger Hunt: Divide into teams, bring a calculator and writing tools, and see who can find the cheapest calorie in the grocery section of the grocery store.

Elder Math: Visit an extended care facility and ask the residents to talk about the math they've used in their lives. Make arrangements to meet with and record the residents' math stories, using video, audio, or notetaking. Edit and share their stories with the class. **Tip:** Write a thank-you note to everyone involved.

The weather's nice and we want to go outside! "Okay, students, we'll go out in teams of two. One member will pick up litter along the roadside. The other will record the type of item, such as can, bottle, plastic bag, etc. (We'll determine these categories before leaving school.) Also record the brands (Bud, Pepsi, Klarbrunn, etc.) too. Ignore gross and dirty items like cigarette butts. Trade off roles halfway through— one person picking, one person recording. When we return to school, we'll wash up and combine our results, then graph our findings. **Tip:** You'll need permission slips, gloves, hand sanitizer, clipboards, pens/ pencils, first-aid kit, and at least two garbage bags per group (one for recyclables, one for trash).

Write your own *Real World Math* book. Each student will interview a family member, relative, neighbor, or school employee for examples of math they do at work or at home. Ask them to talk about how they felt about math growing up, and be sure to get some sample problems of math they use. Record the information, create an answer key, and share your work with the class. Combine your results into a book like this one!